SLAVE SONG

SLAVE SONG

David Dabydeen

Dangaroo  Press

FM
7874
.68
D33
1984

First printed in 1984 by Dangaroo Press.
Reprinted in 1987 and 1989 by Dangaroo Press

© David Dabydeen 1984

ISBN 87-88213-08-0

Australia: G.P.O. Box 1209, Sydney, New South Wales, 2001
Denmark: Pinds Hus, Geding Søvej 21, 8381 Mundelstrup
UK: P.O.Box 186, Coventry CV4 7HG

To Yvonne.

Acknowledgements

The author wishes to thank the British Academy for an award which enabled the publication of this volume.

The painting on the cover is by Aubrey Williams. The author wishes to thank the artist for permission to use this painting.

Contents

Introduction

It is the land of El Dorado, the country of the Golden City of the Prince of Manoa ... to Raleigh anyway who dreamt of setting up an Elizabethan Empire in Guiana. The poetic imagination was kindled, issuing in a splendour of images. 'A region of Guiana all good and bounty,' Falstaff described his Mistress Page. Milton, in *Paradise Lost*, wrote of 'unspoilt Guiana whose Great City Geryon's sons call El Dorado'. In the 18th century, Guiana lost ground to China, Brazil, Tahiti and the South Sea Islands but came back brilliantly with Hudson's *Green Mansions* and Conan Doyle's *The Lost World*, both set in its hinterlands.

Alas, these days the English are literally down to earth bothering only with the extraction of bauxite for their tin cans and the business of sugar refining for their toffees ... the Prince of Manoa is now the brand-name of a box of chocolates.

But to do a Crabbe-like hatchet-job on Raleigh is beside the point for his dream *is* an inexpressibly poignant thing. We are, in literature anyway, creatures of peasant flesh squelching through mud and cane-field, bearing about us the stench of fish and fresh blood. In the moment of our rawness there is recoil, the cry for transfiguration is heard which to the Guyanese is the cry for 'whiteness', for the spiritual qualities of Raleigh's Elizabethan Empire. 'England' is our Utopia, an ironic reversal, for Raleigh was looking away from the 'squalor' of his homeland to the imagined purity of ours whereas we are now reacting against our 'sordid' environment and looking to 'England' as Heaven. All is a criss-cross of illusions, a trading in skins and ideals.

I have only sketched the skeleton of things for the situation is more complex, never a black and white one. Our desire for 'whiteness' is as spiritual as it is banal. On one level it is a craving for mind and soul — the 'savage' wants civilization of the Renaissance kind; on a baser level what he wants is the 'civilization' of cars and fridges — a mere materialist greed. Ironically the white utopianists in English history and literature — Warton, Pratt, Berkeley, Day and others — were reacting against the luxuries and material excesses of their 'civilization' and finding true 'civilization' in the foreign lands. On other levels the cry for 'whiteness' is a sexual appetite. 18th Century white idealization of the Female Noble Savage is invariably bound up with a desire for sexual experience with her, often of a degrading kind, as Fairchild revealed in a study of such literature: sex with the Black meant a liberation from the restraints of civilized behaviour and codes of politeness — that is, a release from the white man's burden of having to appear decent. The white man desired the freedom to indulge in a bestial, fevered sensuality — in what Defoe in the 18th Century described as 'unspeakable acts of copulation'; in what Lawrence in the 20th Century described as the 'hot, fecund darkness of the African body'. The fantasy of dominance, bondage and sado-masochism, of sensual corruption and disintegration, could be enacted upon the submissive, inferior black female. Hence Jonathan Corncob is initiated into the sensual, tropical degradation of taking a 'Negress' straight from the cane-fields, hot, dirty and drenched in rank sweat. If black flesh was bewitching, the same fascination is found for the white woman, from the native point of view — except that this latter lust is an inverse to the former, describable in terms of inspiration, aspiration, assimilation into a superior scheme of things. The poems in this volume (a jumble of fact and myth, past and present) are largely concerned with an exploration of the erotic energies of the colonial experience, ranging from a corrosive to a lyrical sexuality. Even the appetite for sadistic sexual possession is life giving, the strange, vivid fruit of racial conquest and racial hatred. I say a 'jumble of fact and myth' because my purpose is not to provide a sociologically 'accurate' transcript of 'reality' but rather an *imaginative* rendition and reconstruction, a private fantasy.

Most Guyanese are peasant labourers and the majority of these work in Sugar Estates, all owned until recently by a British company, Bookers. Ironically Bookers are involved in English literature (the Booker Prize) as well as in the real exploitation of literature's Noble Savage. They foster the illusion whilst at the same time profiting from the reality.

The peasants work in what are called 'creole gangs' of men and women. The men cut the cane, this being the most laborious part of the sugar and rum business. Guyana, from the cane plant, produces some of the finest rums in the world as Western connoisseurs of the stuff will admit. The workers themselves can hardly afford to buy the bottles that grace the cabinets of foreigners, and they distill their own, a highly illegal operation for it deprives the Government of revenues from the sale of proper rum. The product of the back-yard stills is called 'bush-rum'. Its potency is notorious, causing madness, blindness and sexual impotence if consumed in sufficient quantities — and it is! Bush rum is their drug and their destroyer: in view of the fact that there is nothing else to do after coming home from work in the fields, the men don't mind what its effects are, so long as it gets them merry as well. The women do: severe and habitual wife-beating is a common feature of village life, part of the culture almost, and a large percentage of murders is done under the influence of bush rum. It is therefore an absurd situation: men work, cutting cane and the fruit of their labour, bush rum, is what kills them. It is all suicidal. Why be born in the first place? — but even that was not by choice.

The peasant women have their day, the sexes balance out. Before long, the power of the men has waned considerably due to hard work and hard drinking and the women take over almost completely. They take over the children and control of all business pertaining to the household. The men are physically at an end but the women are still sexually alive, especially in the period of menopause. The male inadequacy creates enormous tensions in the household especially when adultery is an unthinkable step due to cultural and religious conditioning; due too to the quick currency of gossip in a village community. Emotions are pent-up therefore and frustration, instead of being assuaged outside the home, say, in an extra-marital relationship, is directed at the husband. The womb yearns, like Lorca's Yerma's, a battle rages until the old age cools all fires, and death. The children are inevitably caught up in the conflict: they take the side of the mother, influenced by memories of the brutal hand of the father. As they grow up, they can develop an extremely scornful attitude to the father. In the end he is a solitary, beaten figure, an outcast in his own home, with nothing but alcohol to manage his loneliness.

Apart from the drinking of bush rum the business of cutting cane is sordid in itself. There are the dangers of poisonous snakes in the canefields and the inevitable slipping of the cutlass that gashes some part of the anatomy, but besides these minor matters is the sheer physical hardness of the work. It saps all strength, for not only does one have to cut the cane, one has to fetch it as well to punts located in the canal which skirts the field and leads off to the factory. The canecutter, naked to the waist in the tropical heat, chops away all day with his cutlass and towards sunset he separates the cane he has cut down into bundles and takes these to be weighed and then dumped into the punts. Each bundle might weigh up to 100 pounds and he walks to and fro fetching his cane to the punts which might be a quarter of a mile away. He may have to make as many as ten trips to convey all the bundles. It's not a pleasant evening's walk.

If the men are involved in one part of the field chopping down cane, the women may be planting and manuring it in another. The women were also employed in clearing trenches, fetching bagasse, weeding fields, and other such tasks. Their experience of the plantation field was as brutal as that of the men — George Pinckard's 19th Century survey of the West Indies included this passage on the work of the women:

> At one spot, in the course of our ride,
> we had our attention arrested by
> observing a party of four, almost naked,
> females working in a cane field.
> Curiosity would not allow us to pass on
> without devoting to them a moment of
> particular regard. We, therefore, went a
> little off the road to approach them nearer;
> when we found that they were labouring with
> the hoe, to dig, or cut up the ground,
> preparatory to the planting of sugar; and
> that a stout robust looking man, apparently
> white, was following them, holding a whip
> at their backs.

The ritual of cutting and planting then differs from the sower and his seeds in the pre-Christian violence of the operation. Canecutting is a savage ceremony, cutlass slashing away relentlessly at bamboo-hard body of cane; planting is equally vicious, a repeated stabbing into the soil. There is no tenderness or respect for the earth. Male and female are involved in one continuous and conflicting ritual of cutting and planting. Needless to say the conflict continues after work, at home.

This brings us finally to the 'vulgarity' of the language. It is the vulgarity of the people, the vulgarity of their way of life. There is little grace, peace, politeness in their lives, only a lot of cane. If cane dominates life, it also dominates death. If a Guyanese peasant dies and one inquired of his family or friends the cause of death, the invariable answer is 'sugar in the blood'. All non-visible fatal illnesses, whether it be in reality cancer or coronary disease or whatever, are attributed to this mysterious 'sugar in the blood' — meaning diabetes.

The language is angry, crude, energetic. The canecutter chopping away at the crops bursts out in a spate of obscene words, a natural gush from the gut, like fresh faeces. It's hard to put two words together in Creole without swearing. Words are spat out from the mouth like live squibs, not pronounced with elocution. English diction is cut up and this adds to the abruptness of the language: 'what' for instance becomes 'wha' (as in 'whack') the splintering making the language more barbaric. Soft vowel sounds are habitually converted: the English tend to be polite in 'war' ('wor') whereas the Creole 'warre' produces the appropriate snarling sound; 'scorn' becomes 'scaan', 'mortar', 'mata', 'water', 'wata', etcetera. To list the various ways in which English is converted into Creole, with various effects, is inappropriate here and is the business of the philologist, except to say that the speed of Creole speech, the accent with which it is pronounced and the various Asian and African words mixed into it would make it foreign to an Englishman's ear. Writing it down on paper minimizes the difficulties and it becomes quite readable. However the language is primarily oral and the following pieces are meant to be spoken aloud, not read silently, for the tone of them to come through, not merely the abstracted meaning. In an oral language tone creates meaning. Creole is intensely kinetic, and gestures naturally and spontaneously accompany oral delivery.

Another feature of the language is its brokeness, no doubt reflecting the brokeness and suffering of its original users — African slaves and East Indian indentured labourers. Its potential as a naturally tragic language is there, there in its brokeness and rawness which is like the rawness of a wound. If one has learnt and used Queen's English for some years, the return to Creole is painful, almost nauseous for the language is uncomfortably raw, as I said, like a wound. One has to shed one's protective sheath of abstracts and let the tongue move freely in blood again. One has to get accustomed to the unsheathing of the tongue and the contact with raw matter.

In the following pieces I have attempted to exploit the brutality of the language, relating it to the brutality of its users. In *Song of the Creole Gang Women*, the contraction of words like 'work' into 'wuk' (line 1) is typical of the intensity of the Creole language — like the word 'juk' (line 7) which conveys perfectly the sensation of being violently pierced, or the word 'caad' for 'cord' (line 28), the hardening of the sound enacting the sensation of being savagely strapped. The song is made harsh in tone by the monosyllabic starkness of words and by their crude and ruthless rhyming — 'maan ... waan ... baan ... faan ... haan ... saang'. But the language is also capable of a lyrical effect, a sensuous and gentle effect:

> Leh we go sit dung riverside, dip, dodo, die,
> Shade deep in cool deh.

The English fails where the Creole succeeds, particularly in the impossible translation of 'dodo' as 'sleep' for the word 'dodo' means more than sleep and is inseparable from a specific action — the comforting of a child when it is crying by kissing it or patting it until it is quietened and at rest. In addition the simple monosyllables are not crude; they slide into each other — 'dip ... die ... deep ... deh' — a fluidity achieved not by the alliteration but by a simple variation of vowel sounds. The fluid rhythm is further enhanced by simple rhymes like 'leh' and 'deh' ('let' and 'there').

I have also retained the full vulgarity of the language for it is a profound element in Guyanese life: for instance, in the *Canecutter's Song*, I wanted to show the Creole mind straining and struggling after concepts of beauty and purity (imaged in the White Woman), but held back by its crude, physical vocabulary. The canecutter aspires to lyrical experience and expression but cannot escape his condition of squalor nor the crude diction that such a condition generates. So to describe her beauty he struggles to transform vulgar words and concepts into lyrical ones, the result being both poignant and funny: 'the hibiscus flowers in your panties, wet and soft and white' or 'your puss-mouth (i.e. vagina) glows, meshed with light, the sun seeds and sprouts there' (he is trying here to describe the beautiful and fascinating aspect of her blondness, a colour that is strange to his sexual environment, making her unearthly). He has no 'poetical' words because his experience of life under colonialist rule was never 'poetical'. The craving for 'transfiguration' (or 'abstraction') mentioned earlier is constantly frustrated. He cannot escape his words, cannot escape the mud.

The potentiality for literature is very great indeed, for the language, if mastered, is capable of expressing the full experience of its users which is a very deep one, deep in suffering, cruelty, drunken merriment and tenderness. The brief moments of tenderness, usually in sexual courtship or old age, appear all the more profound and memorable because of the norm of pain. It is surprising therefore that very little Creole poetry exists — a handful of folk-songs mostly. With notable exceptions the writers that exist are educated in Western Culture and write like Westerners; or else they write 'tourist' poetry about famous 'beauty-spots' in Guyana, like the Kaiteur Waterfalls; or else they are mere lackeys to the present régime, churning out political stuff, exhorting the workers to produce more for less pay. It's all a fervently stupid patriotism when what is needed is true 'patriotism', that is a recognition and expression of the uniqueness of the people, the particularity of their being.

Song of the Creole Gang Women

1st Woman

Wuk, nuttin bu wuk
Maan noon an night nuttin bu wuk
Booker own me patacake
Booker own me pickni.
Pain, nuttin bu pain
Waan million tous'ne acre cane.
O since me baan — juk! juk! juk! juk! juk!
So sun in me eye like taan
So Booker saach deep in me flesh
Kase Booker own me rass
An Booker own me cutlass —
Bu me dun cuss ... Gaad leh me na cuss no mo!

Caan in me finga, caan in me foot-battam...

Chorus

Dosay an mittae, dosay an mittae,
Booker put e mout on me like pirae.

2nd Woman

Kiss-kiss-kidee! Kiss-kiss-kiss-kideee!
So wind a howl from de haat o bush
Like bird mesh, tear up on twig.
Hear, hear how e'ya cry, cry, how e'ya bleed on de air,
An bruk up over bud aweh hooman, sickle in haan,
Sweep an sway all day to e saang
Babee strap like burden to we back.
Kiss-kiss-kidee! Kiss-kiss-kiss-kideee!

Chorus

Dutty-skin, distress, shake aff we babee
When we reach wataside shake aff we patakee.

3rd Woman

Is true everyting stall, gape, bleed,
Like crappau foot squash jess as e'ya leap?

4th Woman

Everyting tie up, haat, lung, liva, an who go loose me
    caad? —
Shaap, straight, sudden like pimpla, cut free
An belly buss out like blood-flow a shriek?
Or who saaf haan, saaf-flesh finga?
Or who go paste e mout on me wound, lick, heal, like
    starapple suck?

5th Woman

Look a de sun how e fix in de sky like taskmasta eye,
A de coconut-tree dat watch over we like overseer
Treaten fo spill e load on we maiden head...
Me tust, dust an vinega choke me mout, sweat leak over me
    like gutta-wata
Heat a hatch louse in me hair...

Chorus

Leh we go sit dung riverside, dip, dodo, die —
Shade deep in cool deh.

(They move off, repeating these lines with mournful voices,
that gradually fade out. A deep silence.)

For Mala

1st Voice

Yesterday deh pull out young girl from de river tangle —
Up in de net in de fish, bloat, bubby bite —
Up, teet-mark in she troat an tigh:
Was na pirae.

2nd Voice

When deh bin done sport wid she, deh shove bruk —
Top bottle up she front jess fo fun, fo see she squirm
An hear she halla fo Gaad, fo she Muma halla.
She name bin call Mala.

1st Voice

Yesterday she womb bin live an stirrin wid clean, bright
blood
Like starapple inside, full-flesh when yu squash it open
An all de ripe juice run dung yu finga, dung yu arm an
troat.
Now she hollow, now she float.

2nd Voice

Mangoose run aff in de night, yolk a drip from e mout-
kana.

1st Voice

Somebady juta Gaad holy fruit so man can't taste she
sweetness no mo!
Petals o pus she womb put out, dry sticks fo blossom
Under de earth wheh she lie wid she eye open an she mout
dumb.

2nd Voice

Pumpkin dat feed hungry mout now stuff dem guts wid fire.
Five-finga piece by piece drap dung from de sky an bleed in
   de grass —
Mala! Mala! wheh yu deh gal? wheh yu lass?

1st Voice

Gyden na go bear fruit!
Cow na go drap each year!
Wife na go grow big wid belly!
Snake go bite yu foot in savannah!
Alligita go eat yu sheep when dem crass wata!
Hear me cuss like malabunta in yu ear!

2nd Voice

Blackman go pung mata, na mattie head,
Feed dem pickni wid fufu, na mattie flesh,
Coolie grind massala, na mattie bone, stir dhall, na blood.
De air go fill wid curry-smell an roast cassava
Puri an pepperpot
An sitar an steelband go sound wheh gunfire bin a deh.
Lil pickni go laan plant wara-seed na pelt each odda in de
   street wid dem,
An when people kill, dem kill only cackroach, centipede,
   masquita...
Hear me dream like birdsaang in yu ear!

Guyana Pastoral

Under de tambrin tree wheh de moon na glow,
Laang, laang, laang, she lay, laang, laang
She cry, but de wind na blow
An dem wraang an straang
An dem wuk an dem bruk till fowlcack-crow.
Who see who hear when she belly buss, when she mout
splash blood?

Only de jumbie umbrella dat poke up e white eye from de
mud.

Under de tambrin tree wheh de sun na shine
Dem tek up spade, dem dig deep hole, dem hide she from
deh mine.
She puppa look bush, how he hack, how he halla!
She mumma call priest, kill calf, pray Krishna, Christ,
Allah!
Nine mont since dem saach an dem shout, East, West, Naat,
Sout.
Who know wheh she lass, who know wheh foh fine?

Only de cush-cush ants dat lay dem white egg in she mout.

The Servants' Song

White hooman haad like hassa-bone stick in yu gum
Cassava pelt from she eye when she stare an scaan yu,
Dress-up in silk day time, prappa scunt in she silva slippa,
Everyday ting wraang wid she how she fuss
Is like bitch in heat how she yap an spit an scratch an cuss —
'Yu fine me gold ring yet wha me lass?'
'No Missie ... yes Missie ... yes Missie ... no Missie' an yu
   bow till yu neck turn rubba
'Well fine am, fine am, fine am leh me see!
Else me go whip all ayuh nigga tief-man!
Gwan, gwan, gwan! Haak-tuh!'
So we run
An we saach
Wid cutlass
Wid taach
In bush
In backdam
In gyden
In yaad
Till we bruk-up
Till we maad.
Gaad-O-Laad!
We saach kitchen, hall-kana in de house
We saach we hair like we comb fo louse.
Trow way de curry an look in de pot
Trow way de baby an look in de cot
Bu no ring deh!
O me mama, how me friken wha Missie go seh!
Wha we go do? We wring we haan
Saary — saary we bin baan —

Britannia and the Natives.

Till Peta, chupit in e ead since e bin young baai when e fall
   dung coconut tree —
Man chase am, hooman scaan am, call dem husband 'Peta'
   when dem a cuss —
Dis maad — rass, maga — baai seh,
'Leh we go look in duck-battie, me geh mind da ring deh-deh
All night me studyation dis ting an me know e deh-deh.'
He run fowl-pen, pick out waan by chance
Raise up e fedda, skin e leg an peep —
How aweh laugh!
Duck na know wha do am, duck halla, duck leggo waan
   shit —
An ring come out — if yu see leap!
If yu see dance!
All bady hug up a maad baai an shake e haan
Hooman squeeze up e lolo how dem so happy!
An all bady seh, 'Aweh use to mock yu Peta, now aweh go
   laan.'
Den we wash ring, tek am gi Missie
She put am on she finga
Bu we na tell she wheh we fine am.
An when she show aff an she kiss she ring she na know why
   all aweh laugh so loud
She beg we foh tell till she beat we, bribe we, but leh she kiss
   we rass first!

The Canecutters' Song

(The slow throbbing of a drum at long intervals, growing louder and quicker as the song proceeds, then breaking into a wild uncontrolled beating at the last few lines of the song. The men move slowly around the solitary canecutter with slight dance gestures that also intensify gradually.)

Canecutter

White hooman walk tru de field fo watch we canecutta,
Tall, straight, straang-limb,
Hair sprinkle in de wind like gold-duss,
Lang lace frack loose on she bady like bamboo-flag,
An flesh mo dan hibiscus early maan, white an saaf an wet
Flowering in she panty.
O Shanti! Shanti! Shanti!
Wash dis dutty-skin in yu dew
Wipe am clean on yu saaf white petal!
O Shanti! Shanti! Shanti! —
So me spirit call, so e halla foh yu
When me peep out at yu tween cane-stalk, strain me nose
    foh ketch yu scent
Bram-bram bram-bram beat me haat till me friken yu go
    hear —
Bu daylight separate me an yu, an dis mud on me haan
Dis sweat from me face, dis rag on me back...
Yu puss-mouth glow, mesh wid light, sun a seed an sprout
    deh
Me too black fo come deh —

Bu when night come how me dream...
Dat yu womb lie like starapple buss open in de mud
An how me hold yu dung, wine up yu waiss
Draw blood from yu patacake, daub am all over yu face
Till yu dutty like me an yu halla
Like when cutlass slip an slice me leg, an yu shake
Like when snake twist rung me foot, when we cut cane...
So me dream
When night come
An masquita wake up from de bush,
Malabunta move.

Chorus

Baai yu ever dream she drawsie-down!
Baai yu ever wuk she wid yu tongue!
Baai yu ever taste she pokey
Saaf an drippy like baigan-chokey!

A piece of sugar cane.

Slave Song

Tie me haan up.
Juk out me eye.
Haal me teet out
So me na go bite.
Put chain rung me neck.
Lash me foot tight.
Set yu daag fo gyaad
Maan till nite —

Bu yu caan stap me cack floodin in de goldmine
Caan stap me cack splashin in de sunshine!

Whip me till me bleed
Till me beg.
Tell me how me hanimal
African orang-utan
Tell me how me cannibal
Fit fo slata fit fo hang.
Slice waan lip out
Waan ear an waan leg —

Bu yu caan stap me cack dippin in de honeypot
Drippin at de tip an happy as a hottentot!

Look how e'ya leap from bush to bush like a black crappau
Seeking out a watahole,
Blind by de sunflare, tongue like a dussbowl —
See how e'ya sip laang an full an slow!

The Execution and Breaking on the Rack.

Till e swell an heavy, stubban, chupit, full o sleep
Like camoudie swalla calf an stretch out in de grass,
    content,
Full o peace...
Hibiscus bloom, a cool breeze blow
An from a hill a wataflow
Canary singin saaf an low...

Is so when yu dun dream she pink tit,
Totempole she puss,
Leff yu teetmark like a tattoo in she troat!

She gi me taat
She gi me wife
So tear out me liver
Or stake me haat
Me still gat life!

Love Song

Moon-eye
Blue like blue-saki wing,
Moon-eye, all maan in me mine...

Black man cover wid estate ash
E ead haad an dry like calabash,
Dut in e nose-hole, in e ear-hole,
Dut in e soul, in e battie-hole.

All
day
sun
bun
tongue
bun
all
day
troat
cut
haat
hut
wuk na dun, na dun, na dun!
Hack! Hack! Hack! Hack!
Cutlass slip an cut me cack!

Tank Gaad six a'clack!
Me go home
An me go bade
An me go comb
An me go rock
In hammock

Cassava, pepperpot,
Drink some rum an coconut!

...When me soul saaf an me eye wet
An de breeze blow an me eye shet
An de bakle na ga mo rum
Den leh yuh come
An tek me wey, wheh
Chain na deh, wheh
Cane na deh.
Leh yuh come wid milk in yuh breast an yuh white troat
   bare
Wid bangle on yuh haan an bell rung yuh waiss
Leh yuh come wid oil an perfume an lace...

Moon-eye
Blue like blue-saki wing,
Silk frack tumble an splash on me face like wata-fall
An yuh dance an yuh call
In de night.

Elegy

So yu lean over landing, early cole maaning
Old man, yu sick? Is wha do yu? Wha wraang?
An yu haan weak, tremble, an yu mout move
Bu word na deh, an yu eye stare out at de field, laang, laang,
Bu yu na see calf stir an struggle foh suck
An yu na hear high from jamoon tree bluesaki saang —
Is old yu old ... is dah wha mek ...

Snakeneck, Fisheye, Badman, Rich'ed,
Young yesterday, all a dem baais, Tiefman, Blackbattie,
    Goose,
Late late in de night ayuh drink rum ayuh beat drum,
Roast crab, curass, tell jumbie story till maaning come...
Is wheh dem deh? All lay up dem net, all put dung dem
    cutlass, all let dem sheep loose,
All dead!
An Jasmattie beating claat on de riverbank — tump! tump!
    tump! tump!
How she haan straang an she back straight an she bubby
    sweet sapadilla-brung!
Yu memba when yu fuss see she how yu troat lump?
How she young bady leap, leak blood, when yu roll she pun
    de grung? ...

All dem slingshat buss, all dem fence bruk —
Dung, so jackass graze in dem vegetable gyaaden, bird a
    peck,
Fireside crack, an battamhouse, an puckni na blow, bellnay
    na wuk —
An is wha mek...?

Nightmare

Bruk dung de door!
Waan gang sweat-stink nigga
Drag she aff she bed
Wuk pun she
Crack she head
Gi she jigga
Tween she leg!

Dem chase she backdam:
Waan gang cane-stiff cack
Buss she tail till she blue an black
Till she crawl tru de mud an she bawl an she beg.

Dem haul she canal-bank like bush-haag
Cut she troat over de dark surging wata
When dem dun suck dem raise dem red mout to de moon
An mek saang,

Deep in de night when crappau call an cush-cush
Crawl dung hole, lay dem egg in de earth
When camoudie curl rung calf dat just drap
An black bat flap-flap-flap tru de bush...

Wet she awake, cuss de daybreak!

A Rebel Negro.

Men and Women

So me saary.
Bu when yu grow old an yu voice weak an yu mout dribble
An yu foot-battam crack,
Is too late
Foh seh saary.

Bu me still saary.

Kase me drink rum an beat yu
Young saaf wet-eye face.
Kase me gi yu big belly year after year
Nine pickni foh feed, an me run way wid sweet-hooman
Sport all me inheritance whore-house.
Kase yu wuk in de field maaning till night, bruise —
Up yu small haan an yu skin peel in de sun.
Kase when yu sit dung an roll roti, or rock baby in hammock,
Yu na sing glad-glad like odda hooman
How yu mout sour like aachar.

Me come back now, bu now yu old
An yu na know me
How yu mind weak
An yu eye dull.
Bu blood stir in me bady still when me look pun yu,
Like laang-time, when yu was me midnight bride,
Bright, fresh, hopeful, an me lay yu dung dunlopilla bed —
Downstairs dem a beat drum, dem a sing love saang, dem a
   dance in de firelight! ...

An me saary bad!

For Ma

Roll roti! roll roti! roll roti! roll roti!
Curry cookin in de karahee
Bora boilin wid de bagee
Woodsmoke sweet in me nose like agarbattee —
Ayuh wake up wake up ayuh pickni wake up ayuh man
Wid de sunshine in yu eye an de river a flow
An brung doves burstin from de trees an de kiskidees
An de whole savannah swimmin green an a glow!

Wata foh fetch battam-house foh daub fresh bucket foh
    mend clothes foh beat
Wake up ayuh pickni wuk na dun wuk foh duh
Cutlass foh shaap wood foh chap fence foh build dat bull
    bruk dung
Is wha da maan a stretch e haan an yaan foh!
Hear a cow baal in de yaad how dem swell wid milk-fraff
Goat a groan dem want go graze an sheep a caff-caff —
Ayuh wake up wake up time na deh foh cry time na deh foh
    laff
Hen a lay an cow a drap time na deh foh stap!

Slavewoman's Song

Ya howl —
Hear how ya howl —
Tell me wha ya howl foh
Tell me noh?
Pickni?
Dem tek pickni way?
Wha dem do wid pickni
Mek yu knaack yu head wid stone
Bite yu haan like daag-bone?

Is husban mek yu halla gal?
Wha dem do wid maan
Mek yu daub yu face wid cow dung
Juk yu eye an chap yu tongue?
Dem trow am Demerara, feed am alligita?

Muma? Pupa? Africa?
Belly big wid Massa?

Ya howl —
Hear how ya howl —
Tell me wha ya howl foh
Tell me noh?

A Female Negro Slave with a Weight Chained to her Ankle.

Brown Skin Girl

Gwan, gwan America brung skin gyal,
Meet white maan.
Yu go laan
Taak prappa, dress, drive car,
Hold knike an faak in yu haan:
De mud, de canal, de canefield gaan
An me wid ricebowl drinkin mar
Me wid ricebowl tinkin far.

Gwan, gwan America brung skin gyal,
Mek money, mek pickni,
Move smood, stand tall:
Cackroach, kreketeh,
Maskita na deh-deh
Fo bruk yu life fo mek yu crawl,
An me wid fishnet waitin tide
Dreams like bleedin deep inside.

A Surinam Planter in his Morning Dress.

Two Cultures

'Hear how a baai a taak
Like BBC!
Look how a baai a waak
Like white maan,
Caak — hat pun he head, wrist — watch pun he haan!
Yu dadee na Dabydeen, plant gyaden near Blackbush Pass?
He na cut wid sickle an dig wid faak?
He na sell maaket, plantain an caan?
An a who pickni yu rass?
Well me never see story like dis since me baan!

E bin Inglan two maaning, illegal,
Eye-up waan-two white hooman,
Bu is wha dem sweet watalily seed
Go want do wid hungrybelly Blackbush weed
Like yu, how yu teet yella like dhall
An yu tongue black like casrip!
Dem should a spit, vamit pun yu, beat yu rass wid whip!
Is lungara like yu spoil dem good white people country,
Choke an rab, bruk-an-enta, tief dem people prapaty!

So yu tink yu can come hey an play big-shat,
Fill we eye wid cigarette, iceapple an all dat?
Aweh po country people bu aweh ga pride:
Jess touch me gyal-pickni, me go buss yu back-side.'

Song of the Creole Gang Women

The *Song of the Creole Gang Women* is their cry against the sun and against white society; it is also the cry of sexual frustration and the cry for sexual relief. The image of the 'crappau' (a native frog) being squashed by the foot just as it is about to leap is central in conveying this, and in terms of Guyanese life it is an immediate and recognisable image: in the frog season, it is impossible to walk the land without stamping down upon a frog, a very unpleasant and bloody experience. The stench of dead frogs is everywhere, it rankles in the consciousness.

The women bind their waists and abdomens tightly, with cords ('caad') — that is, stripped bark of the troolie tree or banana leaves. This is to prevent strains and belly-aches by keeping the intestines in place for they are continually bending and raising themselves in the process of planting cane. The cords are a sort of makeshift corset. Abdominal pains afflict them terribly in old age if they do not tie up their bellies when they are young and they believe that the power to bear children is also affected without the precaution of 'caad'. 'Everything tied up, heart, lung, liver, and who will loose my cords?' — it is the constant craving and complaint of peasant women.

The squashed crappau and the bandaged, almost mumified women are identified in the song as are their babies strapped on to their backs, usually in a sort of rice-bag sack, their little tiny heads peeping out comically — and pathetically — at the world of cane and at all the strange activity of strange extra-maternal forms.

The female cry is for the release of the womb — 'the belly bursts out like blood-flow shrieking.' (The connotation is of a woman's menstrual flow as a sign of fertility.) This gush differs from the intestinal spill of the squashed frog in that it is vital. The fourth Woman fantasizes about such release, the womb cut open savagely by a 'pimpla'. The 'pimpla' is a gigantic white thorn, a menace to the countryside of Guyana. The use of the 'pimpla' image indicates that although the white man is the menace and subject of complaint (the first Woman cries that 'Booker' cuts into her flesh like a thorn — 'taan'), the women are still fascinated by him: they have a touch of masochism in them and the intensity of their language betrays a surreptitious savouring of their pain. They are both fascinated and repelled by his tyranny as by the squashed crappau which they want to become, yet are sickened by. All this does not however detract from the pity felt for their condition of suffering.

The Chorus sings of the waterside: during their break for lunch the women leave the fields to sit down by the riverside or canal-bank. There they unshackle their babies, drop their cutlasses, loosen their clothes to let the breezes in and bathe their limbs, washing off the cane stains and cane smell. To stumble upon them is like coming upon victims of rape — such is the chaos of attitudes, and the abandon of bodies, and the ache. Piranha ('pirae' — flesh-eating fish) frequent such waters, hence the meaning of their first song:

> Dosay and mittae, dosay and mittae
> Booker puts his mouth on me like pirae

Dosay and mittae are sweet foods made from cane sugar; the image is of the fish attracted to sweetened flesh, to the women with their sugar-cane aroma which washes off in the water. They are fascinated and horrified by the danger — the fish would mutilate their flesh as they wished their wombs to be by the 'pimpla', and as the frog is. The second choric song carries the desire for self-destruction further. They sing of throwing off their babies when they reach the waterside and also of 'shaking off their patacackes' (female sexual parts). The riverside means physical liberation, release from their 'cords', their children and their sexuality. It is a violent death-desire but by the final choric song the thought of suicide loses its hysteria and becomes lyrical, as if what was imagined is now enacted, made actual.

Line 16: The *Kiskadee* is a tropical tyrant-bird named after its shrill call: 'Kiss-kiss-kidee', 'kiss-kiss-kiss-kidee'.

Line 32: The *Starapple* is the sweetest and strangest of Guyanese fruits. When ripe it has a dark purple skin; inside its flesh is the texture of human flesh, raw and running with juice, flesh that like the skin is of a rich, deep purple. The juice literally stains the lips and the flesh pastes on to the mouth and tongue since it oozes a sticky white liquid when sucked. In the song it is used with oral-sexual implications.

44

TRANSLATION:

Work, nothing but work/ Morning noon and night nothing but work/ Booker owns my cunt/ Booker owns my children/ Pain, nothing but pain/ One million thousand acres cane/ O since I was born — stab! stab! stab! stab! stab!/ So sun in my eye like thorn/ So Booker searches deep in my flesh/ Because Booker owns my arse/ And Booker owns my cutlass/ But I'm done with cursing, God let me not curse any more/ Corn in my finger, corn in my foot-bottom.

Dosay and mittae, dosay and mittae/ Booker puts his mouth on me like piranha.

Kiss-kiss-kidee! Kiss-kiss-kiss-kideee!/ So wind howls from the heart of bush/ Like a bird meshed, torn upon twigs/ Hear how it cries, cries, how it bleeds on the air/ And broken over buds we women, sickles in hand/ Sweep and sway all day to its song/ Babies strapped like burdens to our backs/ Kiss-kiss-kidee! Kiss-kiss-kiss-kideee!

Dirty-skin, distressed, shake off our babies/ When we reach waterside shake off our wombs.

Is it true everything stalls, gapes, bleeds/ Like frog foot squashes just as it is about to leap?

Everything tied up, heart, lung, liver, and who will loose my cords?/ Sharp, straight, sudden, like pimpla, cut them free/ And belly bursts out like blood-flow shrieking?/ Or whose soft hand, soft-fleshed finger?/ Or who will paste his mouth on my wound, lick, heal, like starapple suck?

Look at the sun how it's fixed in the sky like a taskmaster's eye/ At the coconut-trees that watch over us like an overseer/ Threatening to spill his load on our maiden heads.../ I'm thirsty, dust and vinegar choke my mouth, sweat leaks over me like gutter-water/ Heat hatches lice in my hair.

Let's go sit down riverside, dip, sleep, die/ Shade deep in cool there.

For Mala

For Mala is about the main heritage of the Colonial Era, which is racial conflict. When the Negro slaves were freed, East Indian indentured labourers were brought in to replace them in the sugar estates, at the middle and end of the nineteenth century. The two races were kept apart and the natural suspicion that exists between any two races or peoples was surcharged in the 'Divide and Rule' policy.

In 1964, a few years before independence, racial clashes took place on an unprecedented scale and a free-for-all slaughter occurred. The high point of barbarity, and the blackest episode of the year occurred at Wismar, a predominantly Negro village at the edge of the Demerara River where in the space of a few hours hundreds of East Indian residents were attacked and killed. The men and children were locked up in their houses which were then set afire. The women and young girls were raped, mutilated and then dumped into the river to die. Only a few survived. It was collective violence and the collective realization of sexual fantasy on a frightening scale — the 'savages' had become *real* savages and certainly not noble.

Line 13: The favourite diet of the mongoose is chicken's eggs, and chickens themselves.

Line 14: To 'juta' is a Hindu word meaning to spoil food by eating it firstly before its proper time, and secondly with dirty hand or tongue. No English translation is really possible. In the song it refers to the rape of the young girl, Mala, taken before her time, i.e. before her womanhood and thus despoiled; also the bodily filth of the rapists.

'To juta God's holy fruit' is to the Hindu a great sin: what is set aside for God (in religious ceremonies) is sacrosanct and to eat it is a great violation.

Line 17: An East Indian stuffed explosives in a large pumpkin and placed it in a river launch. 24 people, most of them Negroes, were drowned or blown up.

Line 18: On March 27th, a Negro activist was found lying unconscious with seven of his fingers blown away.

Line 18: The 'Five-finger fruit' is the name of a Guyanese fig (here connected with the human fingers scattered abroad by explosives, and with the dismemberment, the piecing up and dispersal of Mala). The song is a series of images about food. Feeding is one of the most basic and urgent of peasant activities, sex and spilling blood being the others. Feeding, sex and bloodshed are made one in the song.

   The rape and mutilation with a broken-neck bottle is something that actually happened to one of the victims of Wismar, so I'm told.

Line 26: Massala is an ingredient of curry; 'dhall' is 'lentil'.

Line 27: 'Fufu' is a favourite Negro food made by crushing plantains in a mortar ('mata') and adding various spices. The procedure of making the food is called 'punging mata' (pounding mortar). 'Pepperpot' and 'puri' (line 30) are Negro and Indian foods respectively.

Line 32: 'Wara-seed' is the hard, stony seed of the Awara fruit, used by the children to play marbles or as sling-weapons.

TRANSLATION:

Yesterday they pulled out a young girl from the river, tangled/ Up in the nets among the fish, bloated, breasts bitten/ All over, teeth marks in her throat and thigh./ It wasn't piranha.

When they had finished sporting with her, they shoved/ A broken bottle up her front just for the fun of seeing her squirm/ And hearing her cry for God, cry for her mother/ Her name was Mala.

Yesterday her womb was alive and stirring with clean, bright blood/ Like a starapple inside, full-fleshed when you squash it open/ And all its ripe juice runs down your fingers, down your arms and throat/ Now she's hollow, now she floats.

Mongoose runs off in the night, yolk dripping from the corner of his mouth.

Somebody has spoilt God's holy fruit and man will taste her sweetness no more/ Petals of pus her womb puts out, dry sticks for blossom/ Under the earth where she lies with her eyes open and her mouth dumb.

Pumpkin that fed hungry mouths now stuff their guts with fire/ Five-fingers piece by piece drop down from the sky, bleeds in the grass/ Mala! Mala! Where are you girl? Where are you lost?

Garden will not bear fruit!/ Cow will not drop calves each year!/ Wife will not swell with child!/ Snake will bite your foot in the savannah!/ Alligator will eat your sheep when they cross water!/ Hear my curse like wasps in your ear!

Blackman will pound mortar, not people's heads/ Feed their children with fufu, not people's flesh/ Coolie [i.e. the East Indian] will grind massala not people's bones, stir dhall not blood/ The air will fill with the scents of curry and roast cassava/ Puri and pepperpot/ And sitar and steelband will sound where gunfire was heard/ Little children will learn to plant wara-seeds not pelt each other with them./ And when people kill, it will be cockroach, centipede, mosquito/ Hear my dream like birdsong in your ear!

Guyana Pastoral

The rape and murder of a young girl, told in hard, brutal rhythms, signify the violent aspect of Guyanese existence. The 'jumbie-umbrella' (types of white mushrooms that sprout overnight and are therefore thought of as ghostly things by the people; 'jumbie' means 'ghost') and 'cush-cush ants' convey the grotesque fecundity of natural life which participates in the process of violence, gaining strength by it. Nature itself (the tamarind tree's broad, dark cover; the moon; the wind) seems to conspire in this savagery.

TRANSLATION:

Under the tamarind tree where the moon doesn't glow/ Long, long, long she lay, long, long/ She cries but the wind doesn't blow/ And they're wrong and strong/ And they work her and they break her till fowlcock's crow/ Who sees, who hears when her belly bursts, when her mouth splashes blood?

Only the jumbie-umbrella that pokes up its white eye from the mud

Under the tamarind tree where the sun doesn't shine/ They take up spade, they dig deep hole, they hide her from their minds/ Her father searches the bush, how he hacks, how he's hoarse with calling!/ Her mother calls a priest, kills a calf, prays to Krishna, Christ, Allah!/ Nine months since they've searched and they've shouted, East, West, North, South/ Who knows where she's lost, and who knows where to find her?

Only the cush-cush ants that lay their white eggs in her mouth.

The Servants' Song

The Servants' Song is an example of Guyanese peasant humour, simple and bawdy in a Chaucerian way but more crude. Vulgarity is as natural as a cow-pat, as indicated above. However, on a serious level, the poem does reveal some of the characteristics of village life. For instance Peter, the village idiot — he fell from a coconut-tree when he was young and damaged his brain, a not uncommon village accident — who is the saviour of the moment.

It tells too of the social situation of White Mistress and Black servants — the suffering of the latter, bullied and maltreated by the former in a show of triumph and superiority. In fact in the poem, the servants have the last laugh, as they sometimes did in real life; their resilience and satire are a sort of self-defence, necessary for survival under tyranny.

The hectic search for the ring and the subsequent discovery of it in the duck's anus is (metaphorically) indicative of some of the absurdity of life under Colonialist rule. Only the idiot Peter can cope with the situation; the sane peasants are perplexed.

The Servants' Song is founded upon a very simple Guyanese folk song:

> Missie lass [lost]
> Missie lass
> Missie lass she gold ring [her]
> O find am [it]
> Find am
> Find am leh me see! [let]

It is quite trivial for a folk song ('I've lost my ring! Find it!'), quite trivial that is until one tries to imagine the situation that produced it; until one tries to fill in the gaps that are unspoken, to clarify the hum and buzz of implication.

Line 1: 'Hassa' is a local fish, extremely hard and bony.

TRANSLATION:

White woman hard like fish-bone stuck in your gum/ Cassava pelts out from her eyes when she stares at us in scorn/ Dressed up in silk in the daytime, a proper cunt in her silver slippers/ Everyday there's something wrong with her, the way she fusses/ It's like a bitch in heat the way she yaps and spits and scratches and curses/ 'Have you found my gold ring yet that I lost?'/ 'No Missie ... yes Missie ... yes Missie ... no Missie', and you bow until your neck becomes rubbery/ 'Well find it, find it, find it let me see!/ Or else I'll whip the lot of you nigger-thieves!/ Out, out, out!' (she spits after them)/ So we run/ and we search/ with cutlass/ with torch/ in bush/ in backdam/ in garden/ in yard/ till we're broken up/ till we're mad/ Lord God!/ We search in the kitchen, hall, all corners in the house/ We search our hair like we're combing for lice/ Throw away the curry and look in the pot/ Throw away the baby and look in the cot/ But there's no ring!/ O my mother, how I'm afraid what Missie will say!/ What shall we do? We wring our hands/ Sorry — sorry we were born/ Till Peter, stupid in his head since he was a young boy when he fell down a coconut-tree/ Men shoo him away, women are scorned of him, call their husband 'Peter' when they are cursing/ This mad-arsed, emaciated boy says/ 'Let's go look up duck's backside, my mind tells me that the ring is there/ All night I thought and dreamt upon this thing and I just know it's there'/ He runs to the fowl-pen, picks out the nearest duck/ Raises up its feathers, parts its legs and peeps/ How we laughed!/ The duck didn't know what was happening, the duck screamed, the duck let loose a stream of shit/ And the ring came out — you should see how we leapt!/ And how we danced!/ Everybody hugged up this mad boy, shook his hands/ The women were so overjoyed that they fondled him all over/ And everybody said — 'We used to mock you Peter, now we'll learn.'/ Then we washed the ring, took it and gave it to Missie/ She put it on her finger/ But we didn't tell her where we found it/ And when she shows off and kisses her ring she wonders why we all burst out laughing/ She begs us to tell till she beats us, bribes us, but let her kiss our arse first!

The Canecutters' Song

The hibiscus (line 5) is a lovely white-petalled flower of religious significance to Hindus since it is used in religious ceremonies: sung services of supplication and thanksgiving to Lord Krishna, with priest ('pandit') and congregation. Afterwards sweet foods, fruits and vegetable meals are shared out. These are totally vegetarian ceremonies, no flesh is to be brought in the proximity of priest and worshippers. Whilst this feasting is going on, a white flag is attached to a very tall, freshly-cut bamboo-stick (line 4) and this planted in the yard. A piece of gold, or gold dust (line 3) is wrapped in some cloth and this attached to the bamboo-pole — symbolic payment of Lord Krishna. For the whole community it is a day of joy and feasting, a rare and memorable occasion when there is abandon and plenty; there is dancing, singing, beating of drums late into the day.

The White Woman and such beautifully lyrical religious ceremonies are related in the first movement of the song. In the second movement the perversity of thought, the fantasy of rape is conveyed in non-vegetarian imagery; the *malabunta* (local wasp) and the *mosquito* feeding on flesh and blood, and the *snake*. The 'starapple' (line 19) marks the moment of change from the spiritual to the carnal and obscene, between the first and second movements — it is a fruit belonging to the table of religious festivity but, as explained previously, it is like raw flesh too. The 'baigan' (line 32), like the *starapple*, is of a deep purple colour. The English call it 'aubergine'. 'Baigan chokey' is a special preparation of the vegetable, roasting it so that its insides become semi-liquid, steaming and seedy. In the song, after the imagined rape, the canecutters use the 'baigan chokey' as an image of a spermatic mess. The image of feeding that runs through the song is on one level religious (the ceremonial feasting) and, on another, cannibalistic. Eating is a basic and most urgent feature of peasant life.

The name Shanti is a Hindu girl's name but it is also part of a religious phrase ('Om Shantih, Shantih, Shantih' — the end to an upanishad) and like the starapple it is taken both ways by the canecutters — spiritually and sexually.

The song, starting idyllically, darkens, works up a passion, then culminates in a quick gush of obscenity; the sexual rhythm is paralleled by the rhythm of the drum-beat. The savage imagination of the canecutters is the correlate to the physical savagery of their work. Singing the song is therapeutic since it brings to the surface feelings that are buried under social pressures, and expresses what the canecutters cannot themselves verbalize because of their lack of command of words.

The song is poignant in so far as the canecutters realize that they can never achieve the sort of beauty, cleanliness and inner spiritual strength that are symbolised by the White Woman; from his crouching position among the cane she appears tall, distant, reaching to heaven like the religious bamboo-pole. She is strong-limbed and upright whilst he is weak, bent before the cane. Her eternal bamboo-stillness and steadiness contrasts with his eternal activity: she is removed from life whereas he is steeped in its flux and squalor. His silent call to her (as 'Shanti' — the word means 'peace') is the cry of the soul for release from life, a religious cry. But it is futile. The sunlight separates them, showing their differences, revealing her spiritual, social and physical superiority.

So he will chop her down to size, to possess her in another way, and in the dark, when the differences are not seen.

The fact that she comes to the canefield to watch the canecutters at their brutal work suggests that she is as fascinated by them as they are by her. She wants to be degraded secretly (the long lace frock is temptingly rich, and it hangs loose, suggestively; also the chaos of her hair), to be possessed and mutilated in the mud. The tragedy is as much hers for her desires too are prevented by social barriers. She can only stand and watch and fantasise, then go away. They pause and fantasise too before going back to the cane. Nothing is achieved.

The solitary canecutter sings, voicing the individual fantasy which is the collective fantasy. He is the priest whose words work on them, gathers to a pitch and sparks off a response which is the chorus of lust. The ritualistic song of the canecutters is a perverse replica of that of the Hindu ceremony — both of them, *inter alia*, are cries for fertility.

TRANSLATION:

White woman walks through the field to watch us at work/ Tall, straight, strong-limbed/ Hair sprinkled in wind like gold-dust/ Long lace frock loose on her body like bamboo-flag/ And her flesh, more than the hibiscus of early morning, soft and white and wet/ Flowering in her panties/ O Shanti! Shanti! Shanti!/ Wash this dirty skin in your dew/ Wipe it clean on your soft white petal!/ O Shanti! Shanti! Shanti!/ So my spirit calls, so it cries out for you/ When I peep out at you between cane-stems, strain my nose to catch your scent/ 'Bram-bram, bram-bram' — so my heart beats — I'm afraid you'll hear/ But daylight separates you and I, and this mud on my hands/ This sweat from my face, these rags on my back/ The entrance to your womb glows, a golden mesh of light, the sun seeds and sprouts there/ I'm too black to come there.

But when night comes, how I dream/ That your womb lies like a starapple burst open in the mud/ And of how I hold you down, shake up your waist/ Draw blood from your womb, daub it over your face/ Till you're dirty like me and you scream/ Like when cutlass slips and slices my leg, and you shake/ Like when snake twists round my foot, when we're cutting cane/ So I dream/ When night comes/ And mosquito wakes up from the bush/ Malabunta moves.

Boy have you ever dreamt her with her drawers down/ Boy have you ever worked her with your tongue/ Boy have you ever tasted her womb/ Soft and dripping like baigan-chokey!

Slave Song

The slave addresses his Master (mentally of course). He asserts his manhood, his dignity and his instinct for survival through his surreptitious lust for the white woman, his Mistress. He will not be beaten down or reduced to utter impotence.

On one level his lust is obscene and revengeful: he can cuckold his Master by mentally degrading his Master's wife, dragging her down to his level of existence; that is, he can 'Africanize' her ('totempole her cunt', 'leave his teeth mark like a tattoo on her throat' — lines 32-3). He boasts that he can really act out the role of a cannibal (designated to him — line 15 — by his white superiors) by gaining life at her expense.

But such lust is also life-giving in a more poignant way, as the final verse makes out. His dream of her allows him to survive his condition of squalor — and she does not suffer since his conquest of her is merely mental. She is only a symbol through which to express his desire for life. On a deeper level the emotion trembles on the lyrical (e.g. lines 28-30: the imagined post-coital peace and his deliberate, sentimental evocation of a 'Noble Savage' Utopian ambience), though on the surface it seems disgustingly animal (the images of the crappau frog and camoudie snake). The images of gold within the poem ('goldmine', 'sunshine', 'honeypot', i.e. the pubic blondness of the white woman) play with this Utopian idea cynically ... and wistfully.

There is also an element of comic, mischievous laughter in the slave's celebration of his cock (cf. Medieval ithyphallics) which shows his remarkable strength of character and his intelligence — it makes him heroic almost — for it is humour in the face of utter suffering and cruelty. The gaiety, conveyed through imagery as well as rhythm, undermines the surface obscenity of his fantasy, and adds a further dimension to the psychology of the slave.

TRANSLATION:

Tie my hands up/ Pierce my eyes/ Haul my teeth out/ So I'll not bite./ Put chains around my neck/ Lash my feet tight/ Set your dogs to guard/ Morning till night —

But you can't stop my cock flooding in the goldmine/ Can't stop my cock splashing in the sunshine!

Whip me till I bleed/ Till I beg./ Tell me I'm an animal/ An African orang-utan/ Tell me I'm a cannibal/ Fit only for slaughter or hanging/ Slice one lip out/ One ear and one leg —

But you can't stop my cock dipping in the honeypot,/ Dripping at the tip and happy as a Hottentot!

Look how he leaps from bush to bush like a black toad/ Seeking out a waterhole/ Blind by the sunflare, tongue like a dust-bowl —/ See how he sips long and full and slow!

Till he's swollen and heavy, stubborn, dazed, full of sleep/ Like camoudie snake after swallowing a calf, stretched out in the grass, content/ Full of peace.../ Hibiscus bloom, a cool breeze blows/ And from a hill a waterflow/ Canaries singing soft and low...

It's so when you've done dreamt her pink nipples/ Totempoled her cunt/ Left your teeth mark like a tattoo in her throat!

She gives me thought/ She gives me wife/ So tear out my liver/ Or stake my heart/ I'll still have life.

Love Song

Love Song moves from the wistful idyllic tone of the first stanza, in which the White Woman is conceived as night-cool, night-chaste and ethereal, to the deep self-disgust of the second stanza in which the cane-cutter recognises by contrast his own existence in scorching daylight filth — in other words, from the sensitivity to purity to the sensitivity to grime. The 'dut' ('dirt') he complains of in the second stanza is cane-ash: before cutting takes place the fields are set on fire to burn away the unwanted leaves of the caneplant. The canecutter is therefore steeped in ash as he chops away.

The third stanza sees the intensification of bitterness. Self-disgust gives way to a blasting anger and, at the same time, despair: the line 'work is never done, never done, never done' catches both moods. He becomes worked up, his emotion verges on hysteria and breakdown as he realizes the extremity of his suffering. This mental disintegration is correlated to what he sees as the physical and sexual disintegration resulting from his canecutting labour — 'tongue burnt', 'heart hurt', 'cutlass slips and cuts my cock'.

The fourth stanza sees a sudden shift in tone to one of immense relief and gratitude for the ending of the day, the ending of work and the coming of night. The rhythm changes from its previous incensed throbbing to a childish, joyous jingle.

The final stanzas are sentimental. The Guyanese peasant, when drunk to a degree that eliminates his capacity for violence, tends to become deeply reflective, melancholy, self-pitying, as tender and as helpless as a child. Here the intoxicated canecutter contemplates the coming of the White Woman in the night, a mother-figure who will suckle him and attend to his aching body. She is at the same time the splendidly sexual goddess who will repair the sexual damage involved in his daytime activity of canecutting. Of course she is only the stuff of dreams, but her image and his desire for her sustain him the next day when he awakens to the realities of plantation existence. On the other hand it also makes him frustrated, and his life is a constant flow of desire, and a constant realization of the unreality of his desire. He will remain dreaming in the mud and awakening to the mud, a tragic oscillation between fantasy and reality.

Line 2: The blue-saki is a Guyanese bird of mystical beauty, with sky-blue and sea-blue body and wings.

TRANSLATION:

Moon-eye/ Blue like blue-saki wing/ Moon-eye, all morning in my mind.

Black man covered with estate-ash/ His head hard and dry like calabash/ Dirt in his nostrils, in his ears/ Dirt in his soul, in his anus.

All/ day/ sun/ burns/ tongue/ burns/ all/ day/ throat/ cut/ heart/ hurt/ work's never done, never done, never done./ Hack! Hack! Hack! Hack!/ Cutlass slips and cuts your cock.

Thank God for six o'clock/ I go home/ And I'll bathe/ And I'll comb/ And I'll rock/ In hammock/ Cassava, pepperpot/ Drink some rum and coconut!

When my soul's soft and my eyes wet/ And the breeze blows and my eyes shut/ And the bottle has no more rum/ Then come/ And take me away, where/ there's no chain/ there's no cane/ Come with milk in your breast and your white throat bare/ With bangles on your hands and bells round your waist/ Come with oil and perfume and lace.

Moon-eye/ Blue like blue-saki wing/ Silk frock tumbles and splashes on my face like waterfall/ And you dance and you call/ In the night.

Elegy

Elegy attempts to convey the tenderness, the lyrical potential, of Creole in imagery and rhythm. An old man wakes up on a cold morning to find that there's life around him (natural life — the calves struggling to suck, the blue-saki chirping) but not in himself. His youth is gone, and his woman, and his friends, and nothing makes sense. The atmosphere of death and breakdown of peasant order are conveyed in simple everyday peasant images: Jasmattie no longer beats clothes on the riverbank; her 'bellnay' (rolling-pin for making roti or chipati) and her 'puckni' (peasant instrument for getting the mud fireside started, like a bellows) are in disuse. And the bottomhouse is all cracked for there is no woman to plaster it over with fresh mud and manure. In the early morning the country kitchen is a bustle of activity and the absence of such activity is immediately strange to any peasant. The woman lights her fire, fetches water, fusses among her pots, rolls her dough, calls on the rest of the household to awaken, picks her way among the naked children who squat here and there in the kitchen, in the peculiar way that peasants squat, and who are barely awake, their heads supported dreamily in the palms of their hands. This early morning stupefaction, with a vague sense of the Mother's hectic movements and the smell of woodsmoke, fried fish and fresh dough is a distinguishing feature of any peasant's memory of childhood. In the poem the Old Man awakes and enters into such a childish stupefaction, and memories are unleashed.

As to the male friends of his youth, they're all gone — their cutlasses, their fishing nets, long laid down, and their sheep wandering loose. No-one tends the vegetable garden, a central peasant concern, and wild birds and animals feed and graze unhindered.

The poem can also be read as a lament for the incipient passing of the old rural order in Guyana with the coming of the new urbanized, westernized forms of life.

Lines 8-9: Guyanese country people are often known by their nicknames which reveal their physical or mental features and habits. 'Badman' — man

notorious for violence or wickedness. 'Tiefman' — robber, burglar, etc.
'Blackbattie' — someone with particularly black-tanned buttocks.

Line 15: 'Sapadilla' — a soft brown, deliciously juicy fruit. 'Bubby' —
breasts.

Line 21: 'Bottomhouse' — the space underneath the house perched on
stilts. The 'bottomhouse' is 'daubed' regularly with mud and manure to
keep it smooth and uncracked — a woman's job.

TRANSLATION:

So you lean over the bannister, early cold morning/ Old man. Are
you sick? What's the matter with you? What's wrong?/ And your
hands are weak, trembling, and your mouth moves/ But there're no
words, and your eye stares out at the field, long, long/ But you do
not see the calves stir and struggle to suck/ And you do not hear the
blue-saki's song high in the jamoon tree —/ It's old you're old,
that's what it is.

Snakeneck, Fisheye, Badman, Richard/ Young yesterday all those
boys, Thiefman, Blackarse, Goose/ Late late in the night you drank
rum, you beat drums/ Roast crabs, curass, telling ghost stories till
morning comes.../ And where are they? All laid up their nets, put
down their cutlasses, all let their sheep loose/ All dead!/ And
Jasmattie beating clothes on the river-bank — thump! thump!
thump! thump!/ How her hands are strong, and her back straight
and her breasts sweet sapidilla — brown!/ You remember how your
throat lumped when you first saw her/ And how her young body
leapt, leaked blood, when you rolled her on the ground? ...

All their slingshots are burst, all their fences broken/ Down, so
animals graze unmolested in their vegetable gardens, and birds
peck/ The fireside is cracked, and the bottomhouse, and no mouth
blows the bellows, no hand works the rolling-pin/ And what makes
things so?

Nightmare

In *Nightmare*, the White Woman fantasises about being raped, degraded and mutilated by her Black servants who, according to her warped mentality, are no more than savage blood animals. The nocturnal atmosphere of Guyanese bush-life (stanza 4), one of horrible fertility and death, in some measure conditions her image of the Black.

In declaiming this piece, the canecutter shows his scorn of the White Woman's base image of him, and his tone of narration is full of irony and superior laughter ... his voice lingers melodramatically over the squalid details of her dream to show how extravagant and overdone they are.

The final line glances comically and perversely at the 'aubade' convention in which Medieval lovers lament the coming of the sun which disturbs their secret nocturnal joy. The White Woman awakens, wet with surreptitious sexual arousal and not with terror.

Line 6: 'Jigga': a severe itching and peeling of the flesh as a result of contact with putrid matter.

Line 10: 'Buss she tail' — a Guyanese expression (usually 'buss she tail wid licks', i.e. 'burst her tail with lashes') meaning to beat severely on the buttocks.

TRANSLATION:

Batter down the door!/ One gang of sweaty, stinking niggers/ Drag her off her bed/ Work upon her/ Crack her head/ Give her jigga/ Between her thighs.

They chase her backdam/ One gang of cane-stiff phalluses/ Lash her buttocks till they're black and blue/ Till she crawls through the mud and she bawls and she begs.

They haul her to the canal-bank like a bush-hog/ Cut her throat over the dark surging waters/ When they finish sucking they raise their red mouths to the moon/ And make song,

Deep in the night when crappau call and cush-cush/ Crawl down holes, lay their eggs in the earth/ When camoudie snake curls round calf that's just dropped [i.e. born]/ And black bats flap-flap-flap through the bush

Wet she awakes, cursing the daybreak!

Men and Women

Men and Women deals with the pain of remorse. The peasant, like so many Guyanese peasants under the influence of rum, beat his wife, then later abandoned her with a hutch of children to support, a common fate for country women. Many years later, having wasted his money and life whoring, he returns, but she's old and feeble-minded, a cripple almost, and she does not recognise him. And he's sorry as he remembers the brief happiness he gave her on their wedding night. But it's too late for him.

The poem seeks to represent the whole of Guyanese country life as one of aborted promises, hardships and cruelty — natural and human; the situation only redeemable by individual remorse and compassion.

Line 23: 'Dunlopilla bed' — a Dunlop (English-made, foam-mattressed) bed, the possession of which is rare, and a status symbol, in the countryside of Guyana where people sleep mostly on the floor. Here it symbolises the young couple's hope of marital comfort and wealth.

Line 3: Old country people all have amazingly cracked soles, because of course they're barefooted most of their lives, except on special occasions like when they get married.

TRANSLATION:

So I'm sorry./ But when you've grown old, and your voice weak, and your mouth dribbling/ And the soles of your feet cracked/ It's too late/ To say sorry.

But I'm still sorry.

Because I drank rum and beat your/ Young, soft, wet-eyed face./ Because I made you pregnant year after year/ Nine mouths to feed, and I run off with my sweet woman/ Sport all my inheritance in a whore-house./ Because you had to work in the fields, from morning to nightfall/ Bruising up your small hand, and the sun peeling your skin./ Because when you sat down to roll pancakes, or to rock baby in hammock/ You didn't sing with gladness like other women/ How your mouth was sour like tamarind.

I've come back now, but now you're old/ And you don't know me/ How your mind's weak/ And your eyes dull/ But blood stirs in my body still when I look upon you/ Like a long time ago, when you were my midnight bride/ Bright, fresh, hopeful, and I lay you upon the Dunlop-pillow bed —/ Downstairs they were beating drums, they were singing love songs, they were dancing in the firelight! ...

And I'm truly sorry!